GOD
HAS

KEN HEMPHILL

KINGDOM
PROMISES

DEVOTIONS EMPOWERED BY
BIBLICAL STATEMENTS OF FAITH

GOD
HAS

KEN HEMPHILL

Auxano
PRESS

TIGERVILLE, SOUTH CAROLINA

KINGDOM PROMISES: GOD HAS

ISBN 978-0-578-01512-5

Auxano Press
Tigerville, South Carolina
www.AuxanoPress.com

Dewey Decimal Classification: 242.5
God—Attributes /
Devotional Literature / God—Name

Printed in the United States

I dedicate this book to:

Nancy Hoy and
Linda Lowrance

Women who have encouraged me as
I have labored to advance the kingdom.

They have born eloquent testimony to the
truth that *God Has* prepared rich blessings.

Their strength and courage in the loss of
their husbands has been an encouragement
to all who know them.

In Memory

Harold (Hap) Hoy
1923 - 1997

Jan Lowrance
1945 - 2009

GOD HAS

GOD HAS

PREFACE

Studying God's Word always brings its own rewards. I have been deeply moved by the study of these simple statements that are scattered throughout the Word of God. It is my prayer that they will minister in your life as they have mine. I thank you for your willingness to buy this book and allow me to be your guide as the Holy Spirit informs your mind and transforms your heart.

As always, I am indebted to my wife, who is my partner in ministry and my encourager in this ministry of writing. She brings the order and solitude to our home that makes it possible for me to reflect and write. She is often the source of ideas that soon appear in my books. Our devotional times together frequently become theological discussions which enrich my understanding.

My children are a constant joy to me, and our growing family provides a rich context for writing. Tina and Brett have been blessed with a daughter, Lois, who is as active as her "papa." Rachael and Trey have two children, Emerson and Ward, whose smiles light up a room. Katie and Daniel also have two children, Aubrey and Sloane, who are blessings from the Lord. My family is the context for my entire ministry.

I want to thank Morris Chapman, the visionary, former leader of the Southern Baptist Convention, for calling our denomination to focus on God's kingdom. He gave me freedom to write the things God laid on my heart. All of my colleagues at the Executive Committee of the Southern Baptist Convention have encouraged me in this phase of ministry.

It is an honor to publish this book with Auxano Press whose goal is to provide ministry tools with a balanced biblical perspective to help individuals and churches grow. I can't begin to express my gratitude to Lawrence Kimbrough, my partner in this writing adventure. Lawrence is far more than an editor. He is a friend, colleague, and artist. What he does with a rough draft is a thing of beauty.

This book is somewhat of a new genre. It looks like a daily devotional in its format, but it is written to be "bite-sized" theology. I have attempted to explain each of these great Kingdom Promises in its original context and then to apply it to life. Thus, I highly recommend that you read this book with your Bible open, because the focal passages will have the greatest impact on you as you see them in context. You might also want to consider using these verses as a Scripture memory project while you're reading.

I pray God will use his Word to bring encouragement to your heart. And if this book of Kingdom Promises speaks life to you and ministers to your needs, I hope you'll pass it along to someone else.

Ken Hemphill
Travelers Rest, South Carolina
Spring 2009

GOD HAS
SPOKEN TO US

> **Genesis 3:3** God has said, "You shall not eat from it or touch it, or you will die."

Nothing is more fundamental to our understanding of God than the simple statement, "God has said." In the verse above, we are actually listening in on a conversation between Eve and the serpent, a conversation in which Eve should never have participated. Yet we can learn a fundamental truth that should guide everything in our life. Simply stated—God has spoken, and we must listen.

Jeremiah would later contrast the one true God with idols by indicating that idols were like scarecrows, unable to speak (Jer. 10:5). Even in the first pages of the Bible, where we discover that our God is one who communicates, He is speaking creation into existence. His statements leave no room for any suggestion that the universe is eternally old and self-existent. Nor is there any suggestion that the world came into being by chance. Everything was spoken into being in an orderly manner by God alone.

After God created mankind in His own image, He then addressed them directly, giving them the assignment of filling and managing the earth (Gen. 1:28). Man in the image of God is rational, relational, and responsible, able to comprehend the speech of God. Thus God speaks to man in a way that enables him to hear, record, and respond. The Bible is the written record of what God has said to us. We use words like "revelation" and "inspiration" to speak of the Bible, indicating our understanding that the content comes from God and that man was guided as he recorded the activity of God.

Yet tragically, the first time man quotes what God has said, it is a distorted version. Eve added the prohibition "or touch it," making God appear unreasonably strict. But the fact that God loved man enough to speak to him directly indicates that He wants only our best. His desire to communicate directly and lovingly to man is ultimately seen in the sending of His only begotten Son in human flesh.

GOD HAS
MADE LAUGHTER

> **Genesis 21:6** Sarah said, "God has made laughter for me; everyone who hears will laugh with me."

Perhaps you have heard the old adage that laughter is good medicine. We now have scientific evidence to fortify what we have always known to be true—it is not only enjoyable to laugh, it is actually healthy. Sarah discovered that God was the source of laughter. We serve a God who wants His children to enjoy abundant life.

Sarah's laughter was prompted by the birth of Isaac, her firstborn child. We understand the joy of childbirth, yet in Sarah's case we must know the rest of the story. The covenant to Abraham (Gen. 12:1–2) promised that his descendants would be a great nation. But there was one little barrier to the fulfillment of this promise: "Sarai was barren; she had no child" (11:30). The repetition indicates that her barren condition was a terminal one, making the promise of a "great nation" improbable if not impossible.

Abraham and Sarah struggled to reconcile God's promise with Sarah's barren condition, even though God had assured Abraham that his descendents would outnumber the stars. Some time later, three visitors—messengers from the Lord—arrived on Abraham's land, telling him that within the year, Sarah would bear him a son. Overhearing the conversation, Sarah laughed to herself- as she pondered the physical impossibility of a barren woman—well past childbearing age—giving birth to a son. The Lord asked Abraham why Sarah had laughed and then He asked a hypothetical question: "Is anything impossible for the Lord?" (18:14 HCSB).

Our "God Has" promise ends the suspense that has been building since chapter 12. "The Lord took note of Sarah as He had said, and the Lord did for Sarah as He had promised" (21:1). Her derisive laughter turned into joyous celebration. Her laughter must have played a role in the naming of the child, for Isaac means "laughter." By faith you can see that God fulfills His every promise, which brings us cause for much happiness—even laughter.

GOD HAS
BEEN GRACIOUS

> **Genesis 33:11 (HCSB)** God has
> been gracious to me and I have
> everything I need.

Nothing is more painful than disunity in
the family. Yet God is gracious, able to
restore what has been torn apart.

Jacob and Esau were brothers but also
polar opposites. Esau, the elder son, was to
receive his father's birthright and blessing.
Esau was a rugged outdoorsman while
Jacob was a quiet man who loved to stay at
home (Gen. 25:27). Jacob's name, which
described his grasping of his twin brother's
foot at birth (v. 26), contained the suggestion of God being one's rear guard, but came
to mean "one who supplants" or "deceives."

Deception, personality differences, and
parental preference were all at work in the
affairs that led to disunity in this family.
First, Esau let his rugged appetite overrule
his spiritual values. Then he traded away his
birthright for bread and lentil stew (vv.
27–33). In Hebrews 12:16–17, we find that
by despising his birthright, Esau also

forfeited the firstborn's blessing.

When the elderly Isaac decided it was time to bestow a father's blessing on his elder son, parental preference and deceit entered the picture. Jacob and his mother, Rebekah, devised a plan to trick Isaac into giving the blessing to the younger son (Gen. 27). The deed achieved, Jacob was forced to flee as Esau determined to kill his brother (v. 41).

Jacob was ferreted off to Paddan-Aram to find a wife from among the Israelites. He worked for his uncle Laban for many years, and God provided for him abundantly. Finally Jacob determined that it was time to return home and be reconciled with his brother. But consistent with his character, he devised several alternative plans to save himself and his family.

To Jacob's surprise and delight, however, God had prepared the heart of Esau, who received his brother with great joy. Nonetheless, Jacob insisted that Esau receive the gift he had prepared since God had dealt graciously with him. It was God's generosity that inspired Jacob—and should inspire us—to be gracious toward others.

GOD HAS
MADE US FRUITFUL

> **Genesis 41:52 (HCSB)** He named
> the second Ephraim, "For," he
> said, "God has made me fruitful
> in the land of my affliction."

The story of Joseph is one of the most
beloved of all the stories in the Bible. Yet it
is another story of family intrigue. Joseph's
brothers were jealous of his favored status
in the home, which eventually led to his
being sold to slave traders bound for
Egypt. These Ishmaelites sold Joseph to
Potiphar, an officer of Pharaoh and captain
of the guard. When Potiphar saw that the
Lord had made Joseph successful, he
appointed him his personal servant, putting
him in charge of his household (39:2–3).
When Potiphar's wife was unsuccessful in
seducing Joseph, she falsely accused him
and had him thrown into prison.

Good news! Prison does not shorten the
hand of God. "The Lord was with Joseph
and extended kindness to him" (39:21
HCSB). God enabled Joseph to interpret
the dream of two of his fellow prisoners,
one of whom was restored to his position as

cupbearer to Pharaoh. Later when Pharaoh had dreams that none of his magicians and wise men could interpret, the cupbearer told him about Joseph's ability to interpret dreams. Once again God enabled Joseph to interpret the dream—a forecast of seven years of plenty followed by seven years of famine.

Joseph told Pharaoh to select a wise man who could gather and store the excess food during the years of plenty. Pharaoh recognized that there was no man in Egypt like Joseph. "Since God has informed you of all this, there is no one so discerning and wise as you are" (41:39).

Not only did God bless the work of Joseph, he also gave him two sons. The names of the two sons reflected Joseph's conviction that God had blessed him. The first was named Manasseh, meaning, "God has made me forget all my trouble and all my father's household" (v. 51). Ephraim means "God has made me fruitful."

Whatever your present circumstances, you can be assured that God is able to make your life fruitful, even in the land of your affliction.

GOD HAS
POSITIONED US

> **Genesis 45:9** Thus says your son Joseph, "God has made me lord of all Egypt; come down to me, do not delay."

Do you believe that God is concerned about the everyday events of your life? Do you believe He places you in positions of influence for His own purposes? I am not just talking about places of service in your church. I am actually talking about where you work or serve in your community.

Even after Joseph's brothers had sold him into slavery, God continued to show Joseph favor. He was promoted to second in command because of his visionary plan which enabled Egypt to prosper during a time of worldwide famine. Egypt began to sell grain to the whole earth (41:57). Even Jacob, Joseph's father, was compelled to send his sons to Egypt to buy grain.

In an interesting twist of role reversal, the brothers were now dependent on Joseph for their very survival. When they arrived in Egypt, none of the brothers recognized Joseph because obviously they thought he was dead. During their visit Joseph devised a plan to determine whether God had changed his brothers' hearts. Discovering that he had a younger brother at home, he required his brothers to return to Egypt with their younger brother to obtain additional supplies. When they returned with Benjamin, Joseph put a silver cup in his younger brother's bag, making it appear that he had stolen it. Joseph threatened to put him in jail, but their older brother Judah offered to take his place.

Joseph, no longer able to keep his composure, revealed his true identity to his brothers. They were terrified, thinking Joseph would wreak his revenge. Joseph's response shows us the delicate balance between God's sovereignty and man's responsibility. Three times he repeated his conviction that God had sent him ahead to Egypt in order to preserve their lives (45: 5–8; see also 50:20).

God had promoted Joseph to a place of leadership so that He might use him to provide for the need of His people. How could God use for a greater purpose the position of leadership He has given you?

GOD HAS
Been Our Shepherd

> **Genesis 48:15** The God who has been my shepherd all my life to this day …

Our story of Joseph continues with a family reunion. Jacob and all his family moved to Egypt and were given the land of Goshen. Jacob lived in Egypt for seventeen years. When the time drew near for Jacob to die, he made Joseph promise to take him back for his burial to the land God had promised to Abraham. But Jacob had one last duty to perform. He must leave them his blessing.

You should read all of Genesis 48 to grasp the beauty and solemnity of the moment. Before Jacob bestowed his blessing on Joseph, he briefly recounted how God had appeared to him at Luz and how he had blessed him throughout his life. Upon seeing his grandsons, he reflected on God's goodness. Jacob had not expected to see Joseph again, and now God had allowed him to see Joseph's children as well.

Jacob placed his hands on his grandchildren and blessed Joseph through the blessing of his sons. Jacob used a three-fold invocation of God which is worthy of our attention. He first referred to God in relationship to his forefathers Abraham and Isaac. This indicates the faithfulness of God from generation to generation. Second, he called God his shepherd. We are familiar with this concept from the psalmist but may be surprised to hear it from the lips of Jacob. The third image he used was "the Angel who has redeemed me from all evil" (v. 16).

The image of the shepherd indicated God's constant provision for all Jacob's needs. This memory of God's provision was so vital that Jacob rehearsed it again as he declared that God is "the Mighty One of Jacob, because of the Shepherd, the Rock of Israel" (49:24 NIV).

Have you discovered that God is faithful generation to generation? Have you experienced His shepherding care? Do you know Him as the Angel of redemption? Why not join Jacob in passing along this good news with a blessing for the generation to come?

GOD HAS
BLESSED US

> **Deuteronomy 2:7** The Lord
> your God has blessed you in
> all that you have done.

Sometimes our present circumstances cause us to forget both God's blessings and the commitments we have made to Him. We need someone to jog our memory and call us to personal accountability.

Israel had failed to enter the Promised Land because of their unbelief and their stubborn disobedience (Num. 14). An entire generation died in the wilderness as the people of Israel wandered aimlessly for thirty-eight years. A new generation was now being prepared to enter the land that God had promised to Abraham.

Before Moses passed the responsibility of leadership to Joshua, he reminded the Israelites of God's rich blessing as they traveled from Kadesh to the plains of Moab. First, he summarized the activity of God with the simple but profound reminder—"The Lord your God has blessed you in all that you have done." He then clarified the content of God's blessing with this further reminder—"These forty years the Lord your God has been with you; you have not lacked a thing." The content of God's blessing is His presence, provision, and protection.

Later, in chapter 8, Moses pointed to the blessings of God by reminding this new generation that they had not gone hungry during their journey. The Lord had given them manna each day, teaching them that they did not live by bread alone "but on every word that comes from the mouth of the Lord" (v. 3 NIV). Further, their clothing did not wear out and their feet did not swell (v. 4). Everything God had done to provide for them was to discipline them in the same way a father disciplines his son (v. 5). God's discipline is always purposeful, intended to call us to obedience, reverent fear, and worship (v. 6).

Have you stopped today to thank God for His presence? Do you recognize that everything comes from His hand? Are you aware of His protection? Has this led you to worship Him today? Does your worship include obedience?

GOD HAS
GIVEN US THE HEAVENS

> **Deuteronomy 4:19** Those which the Lord your God has allotted to all the peoples under the whole heaven.

Why is man so easily inclined to worship the creation rather than the Creator? In Romans 1, Paul indicated that creation gives testimony to God, but man exchanges God's glory for mortal images like birds, animals, and reptiles.

Tragically, this problem is not a new one. At Horeb, God allowed His people to hear His voice so they would learn to worship Him alone. Moses explained that—for their own good—God did not permit them to see Him, lest they attempt to represent Him in some form and then begin to worship that form.

The religions of the Ancient Near East contained idols in the shapes of various creatures. The Egyptians worshipped images of animals such as the ox, heifer, sheep, goat, frog, beetle, and reptile. Astral deities were also common. The sun was worshipped as the god Re or Aten.

Israel had been exposed to the worship of these pagan deities while in Egypt and now they were heading to Canaan, where Baal and Astarte were worshipped. Idolatry and the worship of various astral deities would still be a temptation they must avoid. You recall that on one occasion soon after their departure from Egypt, the Israelites had constructed and worshipped a golden calf (Exod. 32).

Moses instructed Israel that they were not to make or worship any representations of creatures or luminaries like sun, moon, or stars, since their God—the one true God—has created all the hosts of the heavens and has allotted them to all the peoples of the earth. Since the luminaries are created by God, they are subservient to Him. Further, they are God's gift to everyone, intended to separate day from night and to mark the seasons of the year.

Surely no one today would make the mistake of worshipping creation! Ever hear of astrology or astrological signs? When man ignores the one true God, he will always worship a lesser god who is no god at all.

GOD HAS
SHOWN US HIS GLORY

> **Deuteronomy 5:24** Behold, the
> Lord our God has shown us His
> glory and His greatness, and
> we have heard His voice.

Many of our songs and hymns speak of
our desire to "see God." No doubt many of
them refer to our desire to see Him in
heaven. But have you ever thought about
what it would be like to see the living God?

In Deuteronomy, Moses prepared a
new generation to enter the Promised
Land. He recounted for this new generation the giving of the law at Sinai. The
Lord spoke these commands to Israel in a
loud voice to the entire assembly from the
fire, cloud, and thick darkness. The people
then approached Moses, declaring that the
Lord had shown them His glory. They had
seen that God could speak to a man and yet
he would live. Still, for fallen man the
presence and greatness of Holy God was
an awe-inspiring, frightening experience.

The people of Israel requested that
Moses serve as a mediator between them
and the living God. "Go near and hear all

that the Lord our God says; then speak to us all that the Lord our God speaks to you, and we will hear and do it" (v. 27).

Sinful man knows at the core of his being that he could never stand unaided in the presence of Holy God. So how can man see God's glory or know of His greatness or hear His voice? We need a Mediator. Do you recall the beginning of John's Gospel? He tells us that from the very beginning the Word existed, and the Word was both with God and was God. Both life and light were in Him. John explains further, "The Word became flesh, and dwelt among us, and we saw His glory, glory as of the only begotten from the Father, full of grace and truth" (1:14).

Only one person could fit this description! Only one was both fully God and fully man! Only one could show us God's glory! Jesus is the Mediator who alone can enable sinful man to see God's glory and His greatness. Here is wonderful news, "As many as received Him, to them He gave the right to become children of God, even to those who believe in His name" (v. 12). Want to see God? Meet Jesus!

GOD HAS
COMMANDED US

{
Deuteronomy 5:33
You shall walk in all the way
which the Lord your God
has commanded you.
}

I was privileged to grow up under the tutelage of a loving father who wanted only good things for me. I must confess that there were times when I chafed at his regulations that seemed overly restrictive. But he told me that as I matured, I would understand that the household rules were only for my good. He was right!

The phrase "God has commanded" is repeated several times in Deuteronomy 5–6. Moses wanted the Israelites to understand that these words and commands were the words of God and not man. Moses was only the mediator of the commandments of God. Like the Israelites, we need to be reminded that these regulations come from God and thus they reflect His character.

Second, Moses indicated that the law was not intended to restrict their lives but would rather lead them to abundance. In verse 33 he mentions long life and prosperity. The law demonstrates the desire of Holy God to have fellowship with man whom He created in His own image.

Third, we should note that blessing accompanies obedience. Blessing is never automatic; it is conditioned by compliance to the will of God. It stands to reason that if God created everything, He alone can inform man how best to live in relationship with Himself, with others, and with creation. But we must define obedience as God defines it. In verse 32 Moses told them that they were not to turn aside to the right or the left. Obedience must be both total and immediate. Partial obedience is total disobedience, and delayed obedience is immediate disobedience.

It is important to note that Moses affirmed the first and greatest law is to love God with all our heart, soul, and strength (6:5). It is this radical love relationship that creates a joyful desire to obey God's every command. We know He is altogether good and giving. Thus when you read "God has commanded," you can know it is a command intended for your good.

GOD HAS
CHOSEN US

> **Deuteronomy 7:6** You are a holy people to the Lord your God; the Lord your God has chosen you to be a people for His own possession.

I love to tell my three daughters how special they are to me. Even though they are married and have children of their own, they enjoy hearing their dad affirm his love for them. Would you love to hear such a message from God?

As Israel was preparing to enter the land of promise, God wanted them to know of His special love relationship with them. God used several terms to indicate how special Israel was to Him. First, they were a "holy people to the Lord." God is a holy God, and thus His people are to embody His character. "Holy" not only relates to behavior; it also implies service. Israel had been set apart for God's use.

But Israel was not only "holy," they were a chosen people. "Chosen" means to be selected for a special task or vocation. Israel was to be the instrument that God would employ in the sanctification of the earth—that is to say, the redemption of the nations. This passage reflects the commission given Israel in Exodus 19:5–6. In that context God declares He has chosen them as His own possession, "for all the earth is Mine." They were privileged to join Him in the redemption of the earth.

Further, God indicated they were His "special" or "treasured" possession. The word indicates how much God valued them as His unique kingdom agents on earth. They were chosen not based on their size or strength but simply because of the great love of God for them. It was His pleasure, His desire, to make them His possession.

Peter used these same terms to describe New Testament believers who believe in God through His Son. "But you are a chosen race, a royal priesthood, a holy nation, a people for God's own possession" (1 Pet. 2:9a). Why were you chosen? "So that you may proclaim the praises of the One who called you out of darkness into His marvelous light" (v. 9b NIV). How long has it been since you told someone about the One who chose you and seeks all?

GOD HAS
GIVEN GOOD THINGS

> **Deuteronomy 26:11** You and the
> Levite and the alien who is among
> you shall rejoice in all the good which
> the Lord your God has given you.

Have you thought lately about all the
good things the Lord has given you? Have
you rejoiced in them?

After years of waiting and suffering
want, it was appropriate (in the context of
Deuteronomy) that every Hebrew family
would celebrate with the firstfruits of their
crops. They were instructed to take some
of the first of the soil's produce they would
harvest from the Promised Land and place
it in a container. They were then to take the
container to the priest acknowledging that
they had entered the land the Lord had
given them (vv. 2–3).

The priest in turn would recite a brief
history of the Lord's gracious activity in
delivering Israel from bondage and providing for them a land flowing with milk and
honey (vv. 5–9). The container was then to
be placed before the Lord as the worship-
per bowed down in worship.

This offering was referred to as the offering of the firstfruits--the first ripe fruit of the early summer. If you continue reading this chapter, you will find that Israel celebrated the abundance of God's goodness with other offerings, which included the third-year tithe for the foreign residents, the fatherless, and the widow.

We can learn from these Old Testament offerings both why and how we can celebrate all the good things God has given us. First, notice that the offerings were brought to the Lord to acknowledge Him as the source of all good gifts. Second, there was a sense of self-denial in the giving of the firstfruits since the farmer would be most inclined to want to keep those for himself. Giving helps us defeat the allure of riches. Third, we should notice that giving was a celebration. The giver, the Levite, and the foreign resident (the recipient of the gift) all rejoiced in the good things of the Lord. Finally, the giving of the firstfruits and the tithe provided for the needs of the less fortunate.

How you can best rejoice in the good things God has given you and your family?

GOD HAS
GIVEN US REST

> Joshua 22:4 And now the
> Lord your God has given
> rest to your brothers, as
> He spoke to them.

Do you sometimes just feel weary in the
battle we call life? If so, you will find this
promise was written just for you.

It took seven years for Israel to complete the task of inhabiting the land God
had given them. The eastern tribes of
Reuben, Gad, and half the tribe of
Manasseh had agreed to fight alongside
their brothers even though their land lay
on the east side of the Jordan. Joshua had
promised that the Lord would give them
rest but required their fighting men to
cross over the Jordan in battle formation
ahead of their brothers to assist them
(1:12–15).

We are told that 40,000 men from these
three tribes went in battle formation in
front of the Israelites (4:12–13). Moses
affirmed they had done everything the
Lord commanded and that none had
deserted their brothers even once during

the entire time of the conquest. Now that the Lord had given their brothers rest, Moses allowed them to return to their homes and enjoy the rest God had promised. But before they could return to their homes, Joshua reminded them that they must be careful to love and serve the Lord with all their heart and soul (22:5).

"Rest" here obviously referred to the cessation of battle, but it is also related to the occupation of the land. The tribes now inhabited the land God had promised them. They were living in His promise! Rest is not the cessation of all our labors; it is living in the promises of the Lord.

Are you resting in the Lord? Do you inhabit the promises of God? Here is how the psalmist spoke of resting in the Lord: "Rest in God alone, my soul, for my hope comes from Him. He alone is my rock and my salvation, my stronghold; I will not be shaken" (Ps. 62:5–6 HCSB). Jesus extended the invitation—"Come to Me, all who are weary and heavy-laden, and I will give you rest" (Matt. 11:28). Want to know victory? Want to experience God's promised rest? Come to Jesus.

GOD HAS
DEPARTED FROM SOME

> **1 Samuel 28:15** Saul answered, "I am greatly distressed; for the Philistines are waging war against me, and God has departed from me."

My mentor, Mark Corts, once preached a message about Saul's rebellion that led to God putting Saul on the shelf in terms of his leadership of Israel. I can remember thinking that I didn't want to do anything that would require God to bypass me like that. This is a sad "God Has" passage, but there is a message here for us.

The closing chapters of 1 Samuel deal with the escalating battle between Israel and the Philistines. The Philistines were attempting to separate the army of Israel into two camps, thus reducing their effectiveness. The issue had been complicated by Saul's rebellion which had led to the anointing of David and the departure of the Spirit from Saul.

Saul's army was in a precarious situation and Saul needed a message from the Lord. He could not receive any help from the Lord's prophets because of his arrogant rebellion. In his desperation Saul turned to the medium of Endor for help, asking her to consult with Samuel on his behalf.

Saul's rationale for consulting with a medium was a tragic one. He could no longer hear the voice of God. He sensed that God had departed from him.

This passage says nothing about a believer losing his salvation. It does, however, speak to the forfeiture of the anointing for service. This was the warning Dr. Corts issued that profoundly impacted my life. I knew I wanted to live in such a way that my life would have meaning and purpose. I wanted to have eternal impact. I still do.

This event in the life of Saul may be the impetus behind David's impassioned appeal in Psalm 51 that God would wash away his guilt and cleanse his sin. After repeated cries for forgiveness and cleansing, David cried out—"Do not cast me away from Your presence and do not take Your Holy Spirit from me" (v. 11). If you sometimes feel that you have forfeited the presence and power of the Lord, read Psalm 51 and follow the directions.

GOD HAS
PROVIDED US PEACE

> **1 Kings 5:4** Now the Lord
> my God has given me rest on
> every side; there is neither
> adversary nor misfortune.

Do you ever feel a need for rest? That's
a rather silly question! We all need to
rest—body and soul. The pace of life has
intensified, and sufficient rest has become
an even more precious commodity.

In the above verse King Solomon
celebrated the rest that the Lord had given
him. If you read the context, you will find
that the "rest" he enjoyed was the freedom
from the constant warfare that had marked
his father David's reign.

This passage begins with the note that
Hiram, king of Tyre, had sent his servants
to assure Solomon that he intended to
continue the strong diplomatic relationship
he had established with David. Hiram had
supplied David with the timber, carpenters,
and stonemasons to build his residence in
Jerusalem.

Solomon responded to the overture of
Hiram with the reminder that his father

had desired to build a temple for the name of the Lord but had been prevented from doing so because of the constant warfare that surrounded him (v. 3). Now that the Lord had given him rest, Solomon could begin construction on the temple that his father had so longed to construct for the glory of God.

When Hiram heard of Solomon's desire to construct the temple, he greatly rejoiced and said, "Blessed be the Lord today" (v. 7). Solomon's wisdom, reflected in his focus on a kingdom priority accompanied by God's provided "rest," had caused a pagan king to recognize the activity of God.

This is a wonderful story, but you may be wondering what it has to do with you today. First, we should note that it points to God's faithfulness in providing both rest and the resources for the temple. You can be assured that God will be faithful to provide for your needs. Second, we must ask ourselves if we desire rest so that we can focus on kingdom priorities. Do you seek peace and rest so you can accomplish something great for the King?

GOD HAS
HEARD WHAT IS SAID

> **2 Kings 19:4** Perhaps the Lord your God will hear all the words of Rabshakeh . . . and will rebuke the words which the Lord your God has heard.

My grandfather was nearly deaf, and we children had to shout in his ears to be heard. We quickly discovered, however, that if we said something we didn't intend for him to hear, he seemed to have nearly bat-like radar. Do you sometimes despair, wondering if the Lord has heard?

Israel and King Hezekiah were reeling from defeat at the hands of the Assyrian army. The Assyrian king Sennacherib sent his spokesmen to deliver a taunting message to the representatives from Israel, warning them not to trust in Egypt for any assistance (18:21), telling them they could not trust in the words of their king (v. 32), then listing the conquests of Sennacherib over other pagan gods saying, "So how is the Lord to deliver Jerusalem?" (v. 35 HsCSB).

The men of Hezekiah had been instructed to keep silent during the report of the

Rabshakeh. They did not respond to the taunting report. They did, however, relate the message to Hezekiah. And his response was immediate! "He tore his clothes, covered himself with sackcloth and entered the house of the Lord" (19:1), repenting of his sins and seeking God's face. He then sent one of his servants to tell the prophet Isaiah what the pagan king had said about the one true God, comparing Israel's condition to that of a pregnant woman who does not have the strength to give birth.

Hezekiah realized that his only hope was that the one true and living God would grant them miraculous deliverance. Notice that the reference to God's "hearing" in this kingdom promise actually relates to the taunting words of a pagan king. Isaiah sent the servants back with good news that the Lord had indeed heard the blasphemous words and was about to act on behalf of His own name.

When you feel defeated and think the world is spiraling out of control, you must remember that the Lord has heard and knows everything. He can be trusted to set everything right.

GOD HAS
POWER TO HELP

> **2 Chronicles 25:8** God has
> power to help and to
> bring down.

Our desire to assist God is a demonstration of our lack of understanding of His great strength. Yet we find ourselves time and again attempting to accomplish spiritual gain through our own might.

Amaziah became king of the two tribes of Judah when he was twenty-five years of age. The chronicler provides an interesting assessment of his reign—"He did what was right in the Lord's sight but not completely" (25:2 HCSB). You will see the relevance of this statement in the following account.

Amaziah wanted to once again subdue the Edomites, who had rebelled from the dominion of Judah. His resolve was demonstrated by the marshalling of a large army, beginning with 300,000 choice men from the tribes of Judah and Benjamin. Thinking this to be insufficient for his needs, he hired 100,000 mercenaries from Israel for 7,500 pounds of silver.

What Amaziah had failed to understand, however, was that this reliance on
his own military might had led him to make
an ungodly alliance. An unnamed prophet
warned him not to depend on these people
who had abandoned the one true God for
idolatrous worship. If he did go to battle
with them, the prophet said the Lord
would not be with him. In fact, God would
bring him down. What Amaziah failed to
understand was that God has the power
both to help and to bring down.

The sin of Amaziah was not simply
making an unholy alliance with idolatrous
Israel; it was trusting in the might of his
army rather than trusting in God. When
headed for battle, his first thought was to
assemble an army rather than to pray.

We are often guilty of thinking we can
do something great for God by our own
strength or ingenuity. We make our plans,
marshal our resources, and ignore the
promises of God who has the power to
help. I don't want God to have to say that
Ken did what was right in His sight, "but
not completely."

GOD HAS
GIVEN US NEW LIFE

> **Ezra 9:8 (HCSB)** Even in our
> slavery, God has given us new
> life and light to our eyes.

The enormity of our sin can cause us to feel so unworthy of God's grace that we see no way of return. This feeling of shame can lead to a condition of spiritual slavery where we feel trapped with no hope. The prayer of Ezra, which provided hope for captive Israel, will give you hope today.

The book of Ezra chronicles the return of Israel from Babylonian captivity. It begins with the edict of Cyrus, the Persian King, who permitted a remnant of Israel to return to the Promised Land and rebuild the temple. The rebuilding of the temple faced opposition, so work on the temple ceased for a season. King Artaxerxes sent Ezra the priest to lead a spiritual reformation in Israel (7:25–26).

Ezra was greeted with disturbing news. The leaders told him that intermarriage with the pagans and the resulting idolatrous practices had not been abandoned by the people, the priests, or the Levites (9:1–2). Ezra was so grieved by the news that he tore his tunic, pulled out some of his hair, and sat down devastated.

Then he took three interrelated actions: he got up from his humiliation, fell on his knees, and spread out his hands to the Lord. In other words, the key to overcoming his devastation was prayer. In his prayer he acknowledged the corporate sin of Israel, confessing that he was ashamed to lift his face toward heaven.

I love the opening words of verse 8—"But now for a brief moment grace has been shown from the Lord our God, to leave us an escaped remnant." God had shown grace by allowing a remnant to return and gave them life even in the days of slavery. Ezra was given hope by focusing on the merciful nature of God who made a way for restoration.

When you are crushed by the enormity of your sin, follow the example of Ezra. Get up from your humiliation, fall on your knees, and spread out your hands to the Lord. He wants to deliver you from slavery and give you new life through His Son.

GOD HAS
CREATED US

> **Job 33:4** The Spirit of God has made me, and the breath of the Almighty gives me life.

There are certain fundamental truths that impact how we view all of life. One such issue is our origin. Once we acknowledge that God has made us and given us life, it alters how we view all other realities about life itself.

In the opening verses of the book of Job, the narrative unexpectedly switches to a scene in the heavenlies where the Lord and Satan are conversing about the people on earth, specifically Job. Satan concludes that Job fears God because he has been blessed and protected by God. Satan asserts that if Job were to face adversity, he would curse God to His face (1:11).

As the book unfolds we discover that Job soon loses everything including his health. But as the blessings are taken away one after the other, Job remains faithful to the Lord. His wife and several friends offer him advice on why such difficulties have befallen him and what he should do about it. Much of their advice is based on the popular view that bad circumstances in life are directly caused by sin. Thus many of their speeches give the impression they are lecturing Job about his shortcomings.

Elihu was younger than the three friends who had tried to convince Job that he had lived a thoroughly reprobate life and needed to repent. He expressed anger at Job for wanting to justify himself rather than God (32:2). But he was also angry at the friends because they had condemned Job without sufficient evidence (v. 3).

Elihu had waited until last to speak, perhaps because of his youth. His speech, however, is less arrogant and presumptuous than that of the other three friends. He begins with a fundamental truth: the Spirit of God has made us, and thus we are all equal before God (33:8). Elihu's speech is lengthy, but throughout he focuses on the greatness of God.

When we rightly understand that God has made us, we understand (like Elihu) that all of our life is in His hands.

GOD HAS
BLESSED US FOREVER

> **Psalm 45:2** Grace is poured upon Your lips; therefore God has blessed You forever.

We use the terms "blessing" and "blessed" rather casually. We may speak of being "blessed" by a song or by a favor done for us by another. But we understand that while a person may be the instrument through which a blessing comes, all blessings actually come from God. If we agree we have been blessed by God, what is the evidence of that blessing?

Psalm 45 is referred to as a "love song" or a "royal wedding song." It may have been written for King Solomon. The writer admits that he is somewhat overwhelmed as he attempts to address such a noble theme to the king (v. 1).

The psalmist sees the king as the most handsome of men, and notes that "grace is poured upon Your lips" (v. 2). The gracious speech of the king is the evidence that God has blessed him forever. The intent of the words spoken by one who has been blessed is to bless others, and thus their words communicate and contain grace.

You may recall that when Jesus read the scroll of the prophet Isaiah in the synagogue in Nazareth, He declared to the crowd, "Today this Scripture has been fulfilled in your hearing" (Luke 4:21). What was the immediate response? "All were speaking well of Him, and wondering at the gracious words which were falling from His lips" (v. 22).

Read Psalm 45 and you will notice that on three occasions the psalmist used the term "forever" in relationship to the king. He is blessed forever (v. 2), His throne is forever (v. 6), and the peoples will praise Him forever (v. 17). You may find this ascription of deity to the King surprising. This Old Testament enigma of an anointed King who is God and yet worships God awaits its ultimate fulfillment and resolution in Jesus. Thus it is appropriate to see here a picture of Christ and His bride, the church.

While you celebrate that picture, may I ask you if your speech tells others that you have been blessed?

GOD HAS
ASCENDED ON HIGH

> **Psalm 47:5** God has ascended with a shout, the Lord, with the sound of a trumpet.

Have you ever attended or watched a presidential inauguration? Pretty impressive, to say the least! A presiential inauguration is like a regal celebration. Few monarchies remain today, but any event that involves royalty is replete with stunning pageantry. Psalm 45 speaks of a royal coronation of the King over all the earth.

The psalmist pictures God ascending His throne amid shouts of acclamation, sounds of trumpets, and songs of praise. The call to praise is based on the singular truth that God is the King of all the earth and reigns over all the nations (vv. 7–8). The psalmist depicts the Great King as seated on His holy throne (v. 8). This "God Has" declaration is a prophetic statement of a future certainty.

You may recall that the apostle Paul spoke of this royal coronation day, when "at the name of Jesus every knee will bow, of those who are in heaven and on earth and under the earth, and that every tongue will confess that Jesus Christ is Lord, to the glory of God the Father" (Phil. 2:10–11).

John, in the final book of the Bible, gives us a visual picture of the coronation, with the kings of the earth bowing before the only true King. He speaks of the New Jerusalem, indicating that it has no physical sanctuary in it, "for the Lord God the Almighty and the Lamb are its temple" (Rev. 21:22). The glory of God illuminates the new city, and the Lamb is its lamp. "The nations will walk by its light, and the kings of the earth will bring their glory into it" (v. 24).

The coronation prophesied by the psalmist and pictured in Revelation is an absolute certainty. There are times when we see the chaos and confusion of our world, with nations at war and earthly rulers rising and falling. We can become discouraged by it all. But this promise should not only console us, it should call us to action. If we know and serve this King, we should join Him in His kingdom activity as He reclaims the nations for Himself—the King over all the earth.

GOD HAS
SHONE FORTH

> **Psalm 50:2** Out of Zion,
> the perfection of beauty,
> God has shone forth.

Do you ever watch courtroom dramas on television? The bailiff announces the coming of the presiding judge with great solemnity. Then the judge, wearing his black gown, ascends to the bench to begin the trial. The psalmist allows us to glimpse into the heavenly courtroom where God judges His own people.

Verse 1 contains the declaration of the one who will bring judgment—"The Mighty One, God, the Lord, has spoken." Three names—El, Elohim, and YHWH—are heaped one upon the other to indicate that this Judge alone is qualified to execute perfect judgment. As he descends from Zion, he is described as the perfection of beauty. Because the place of God's presence is a glorious one, it is appropriate to say that "God has shone forth" in glory. The psalmist can only compare it to the rising sun.

Yet His beauty does not negate that He is coming in judgment. "Fire devours before Him, and it is very tempestuous around Him" (v. 3). These descriptions cause us to think about His appearance on Mount Sinai in the giving of the Law—great and glorious, too holy for man to behold. The judge calls upon all of heaven and earth as a witness against His people (v. 4). The whole of God's created order has seen both human failing and the righteousness of God, and thus has become a reliable witness.

He then calls upon His people, "Offer to God a sacrifice of thanksgiving and pay your vows to the Most High" (v. 14). Israel had become careless and ritualistic in their worship. The Judge is calling them to genuine worship and holy conduct that is befitting their righteous King.

It is true that believers will not stand before the "great white throne" judgment. The penalty for our sins has already been paid. But both testaments speak to a judgment of believers for the quality of their life and service to the King. Are you prepared for God to shine forth?

GOD HAS
LOOKED DOWN

> **Psalm 53:2** God has looked down from heaven upon the sons of men to see if there is anyone who understands.

Watching the evening news can be downright depressing. Hardly an evening goes by that we are not confronted by scenes of killing and pillaging around the globe. It makes us understand the cry of David declaring that God has looked down to see "if anyone understands."

This verse assures us that our God is not a distant god unconcerned about the people of His creation. Rather He carefully investigates the human race to see if there is anyone who is prudent.

People sometimes pose the question, "If a righteous God exists, why is there such manifest evil in the world?" David answers that very question in verse 1: "The fool has said in his heart, 'There is no God.' They are corrupt, and have committed abominable injustice." The description of a fool is one who denies the existence of God. But this denial is not just a verbal declaration.

It is a matter of the conduct of one's life. A person might declare that he or she believes in God, but then live as if He does not look down from heaven or care about His own creation. If one concludes God does not exist, then life contains neither purpose nor accountability. Man, drawn and corrupted by his fallen nature, makes no place for God (v.3).

You might ask, "What is the purpose of God's downward gaze?" David echoes the heart of God when he cries out for the establishment of God's kingdom. He longs for the day when God restores His people and Israel will be glad (v. 6).

Paul quoted this Psalm in Romans 3:10–12 to demonstrate the guilt of all mankind before a holy God. His conclusion answers the cry of David's heart: "For all have sinned and fall short of the glory of God, being justified as a gift by His grace through the redemption which is in Christ Jesus" (3:23–24).

God not only looked down upon man's depravity, He came down in the person of Jesus to provide the answer for our sin.

GOD HAS
SPOKEN IN HOLINESS

> **Psalm 60:6** God has spoken in
> His holiness: "I will exult."

We have a habit of getting ourselves
into trouble by running ahead of God. We
make our own plans, discover they are not
working, and then turn to God for help.

The context of this psalm is David's plea
for God's help against his enemies. You can
read about it in 2 Samuel 8. While David
was busy waging war in the north against
the Arameans, Edom invaded Judah from
the south. Some commentators argue that
David's military success had caused him to
invade the Arameans, leaving his own
young kingdom at unnecessary risk. In any
case, Joab met the attack and achieved
victory. It is into this context that David
declares that God has spoken in His
holiness.

The psalm begins with an admission
that God has been displeased with them
and has broken them down. They see their
military losses as signs of God's displea-

sure. He has made the earth tremble and has shown His people hard things.

But no matter the cause of their defeat, God has given them a banner or rallying point. In ancient warfare a banner was often a metal insignia that could be lifted high on a staff to call the troops together. The banner to be unfurled is the banner of prayer. God's people will depend upon God's truth and pray that they might be delivered by His right hand.

David rejoices in the understanding that "God has spoken in His holiness." In other words, God has spoken based on His attributes. The integrity of His Word is based on the integrity of His character. This became the firm foundation of David's hope. Listen to David's conclusion—"Give us help against the adversary, for deliverance by man is in vain. Through God we shall do valiantly" (vv. 11–12).

Isn't it wonderful to know that God's promises are based upon His character? If you find yourself reeling from defeat, do like David and rally around God's banner of prayer. Trust in His character and trust in His Word.

GOD HAS
LISTENED TO OUR PRAYER

> **Psalm 66:19** Certainly God has
> heard; He has given heed to the
> voice of my prayer.

Surveys indicate that prayer is a topic of great interest to most Christians. Tragically, other surveys reveal that we are somewhat casual in our practice of prayer. I wonder why? Do we believe that prayer matters? Does God actually listen to our prayers? I suppose we have all asked similar questions. Fortunately, the psalmist provides a positive answer for all who desire a more intimate prayer life.

This psalm begins with a call for all the earth to worship and praise the Lord through joyful shouting, singing, and speaking. The reason? "Come and see the works of God, who is awesome in His deeds" (v. 5), such as their deliverance at the Red Sea. Yet the psalmist acknowledges that Israel had also been tested by the Lord. He speaks of having burdens on their backs and men riding over their heads (vv. 11–12). Nevertheless, God had brought them through the fire and water and had brought them out to abundance.

Perhaps this text reminds you of the promise in 1 Corinthians 10:13 where Paul tells us God will never test us beyond our ability, but will always provide a way to bear it. The difficulties of our life serve to test and refine our faith.

The writer calls for everyone who fears God to listen to what He has done for us. He then celebrates the truth that God has listened and paid attention to our prayer. He praises God for His faithfulness: "Blessed be God, who has not turned away my prayer nor His lovingkindness from me" (v. 20). He indicates that a necessary prerequisite of answered prayer is a clean heart. Isaiah would later tell his listeners that their sin had built barriers between them and God (59:2).

What lessons can we learn that will help us gain the confidence that God listens to our prayers? 1) Always begin with praise. 2) Remember past events where you have seen the hand of God. 3) Confess your sins and cleanse your heart. 4) Pray continually with confidence.

GOD HAS
COMMANDED STRENGTH

> **Psalm 68:28** Your God has commanded your strength; show Yourself strong, O God, who have acted on our behalf.

An emphasis on physical strength is common among most athletes. But recent breakthroughs in strength training have taken this to a new level. Even athletic events not normally connected with strength, such as driving a race car or a golf ball, now have their own specific training regimen. Even persons who are not athletically inclined are encouraged to incorporate elements of strength training into their regular exercise program. Yes, muscular strength is important to our overall well-being.

But today's promise reminds us that God has "commanded" our *spiritual* strength. This kingdom promise is found in a psalm that recalled the forward march of Israel from Sinai toward Canaan. It may have been composed to celebrate when David returned the Ark of the Covenant to Mount Zion (2 Sam. 6:12–16).

As you might anticipate, the psalmist describes God's power in majestic terms. He pictures Him as the God who rides on the clouds and through the desert (v. 4). The earth trembles and the skies pour rain before Him, "the God of Israel" (v. 8). Kings of armies flee before Him whose chariots number in the thousands of thousands (vv. 12, 17).

You may, however, be surprised to discover that His power is also related to His care for the fatherless and widows (v. 5). He is a God who provides homes for the homeless and leads prisoners to prosperity (v. 6). Yes, He is a majestic King.

Isn't it wonderful to know that our God, who is the majestic King of kings, commands our strength? Whatever strength we have comes from Him. Thus we have no reason either to fear or to boast. Paul would state this same truth by saying, "I can do all things through Him who strengthens me" (Phil. 4:13).

Are there times when you don't feel very strong? Feelings can lie to you. Base your actions on God's promises. He has commanded your strength!

GOD HAS
MADE THINGS BEAUTIFUL

> **Ecclesiastes 3:11** (NIV) He has
> made everything beautiful in its
> time. He has also set eternity in
> the hearts of men.

Do you ever wonder, "What good is all
my hard work? What do I get for all my
labor? Life has to be about more than a
paycheck." If so, you are in good company.
Solomon, the wise king of Israel, wrote
about the purpose of life and work, and
was forced to conclude that life has a
certain futility about it.

But ultimately Solomon was no pessi-
mist. Moved by the Holy Spirit, he con-
templated life in the context of eternity. He
was aware that man is on a divine quest for
both meaningful and eternal significance.
He recognized that there must be more to
life than the few short years of earthly
existence.

Solomon began chapter 3 with the
affirmation that when you take the long
view, life has structure and meaning.
"There is an appointed time for everything.
And there is a time for every event under

heaven" (v. 1). He then declared that he had observed the tasks which God has given to man. Have you ever thought about your work at home or your profession as a God given task? It is! This changes everything about how and why we work.

Solomon underlined three truths which help us find purpose in life and fulfillment in our work. 1) God has made everything "appropriate," "beautiful," or a "source of delight." God is a happy God who wants His children to enjoy life. Thus in His sovereign care He has given meaning and purpose to everything. 2) God has also put eternity in our hearts. Man longs for his life to have an ultimate significance, just as he longs for life after death. God has put that desire there. 3) Finally, no one can fully comprehend the work of God. There is a mystery to life that eludes man because he is finite and thus his vision is limited.

What is man to do to find meaning? He must know the eternal God through His Son. This eternal perspective will allow him to rejoice and do good through the labor God has given him.

GOD HAS
GIVEN RICHES AND WEALTH

> **Ecclesiastes 5:19** For every man
> to whom God has given riches and
> wealth, He has also empowered
> him to eat from them.

In a televised interview, pastor Rick
Warren asked both 2008 presidential
candidates to define "wealthy." Neither was
very successful in determining a dollar
amount because wealth must always be
placed in context. Rick joked about the
context of California and the higher cost of
living. Yet if we place this question in a
global context, anyone with the money to
afford anything beyond the necessities of life
would be considered wealthy. What then
does God tell us about wealth?

We must acknowledge it is God who has
given us the life, strength, and ability to
work, and thus He has given us both riches
and wealth, whatever the amount. This
understanding is critical to a proper view of
financial resources.

When Moses was preparing Israel to
enter the Promised Land, he reminded them:
"You shall remember the Lord your God, for

it is He who is giving you power to make wealth, that He may confirm His covenant which He swore to your fathers, as it is this day" (Deut. 8:18). This brought up two issues that were at stake for the people in relation to the abundance of the Promised Land. First, they would be so focused on building their houses and multiplying their holdings, they would be tempted to forget God's commands (8:11–14). Second, they might proudly argue that their power and strength had made them wealthy (8:17). Truly, wealth can be both deceptive and destructive.

So why does God desire to give us resources? The writer of Ecclesiastes mentions the first reason, and that is to provide for our needs and pleasure. Yet there is more, and Deuteronomy 8 helps us fill in the gaps. God desires to confirm His covenant. His blessing was never intended to be consumed, but always to be conveyed. Thus He desires to provide us with sufficient resources to meet our needs and to join Him in providing for the less fortunate and to reach the nations. As you contemplate your wealth, are you using it according to His desire?

GOD HAS
APPROVED OUR WORKS

> **Ecclesiastes 9:7** Eat your bread
> in happiness and drink your wine
> with a cheerful heart; for God has
> already approved your works.

In our promises from Ecclesiastes, we
have been focusing on our work and our
wealth. Let's look at one more "God Has"
promise that relates to life, wealth, and
work.

In verses 7–9, Solomon looked at the
ordinary events of life such as eating,
drinking, and enjoying "the woman whom
you love all the days of your fleeting life."
Solomon, who accumulated great wealth
and led Israel as their king, advises that we
enjoy life itself. Read the verses leading up
to this promise, and you will find that
Solomon first underlines two absolutes
concerning life. First, we cannot predict
whether we will face adversity or prosperity, and it is likely that we will know both
(vv. 1–3). Second, life is short and death is
certain for everyone (vv. 4–6).

Solomon advises us to enjoy three
specific areas of life—feasting, our spouse,

and our work or occupation. In verse 7 he speaks of food and wine in the context of happiness and a cheerful heart. He elaborates on the theme of joy in verse 8 when he speaks of white garments and oil for our head, both of which symbolize joy.

His recommendation that we enjoy our spouse is placed in the context of our "fleeting life." A few years ago a rather poignant song entitled "The Cat's in the Cradle" became quite popular. It spoke of a busy father who ignored his son until with time the table was turned and the son ignored the needs of the elderly father. We must make each moment count with those we love. This is a gift of God.

Finally he speaks of enjoying our work or vocation (v. 10). He reminds us that death will put an end to our earthly labors, thus we must enjoy them in this life as a gift of God.

Solomon's advice is based on the truth that God has already approved your works. Possessing God's gifts and being allowed to enjoy them is evidence of His prior approval. In other words, we serve a God who wants us to have an abundant life.

GOD HAS
GIVEN US WORDS

> **Isaiah 50:4** The Lord God has given Me the tongue of disciples, that I may know how to sustain the weary one with a word.

Do you ever find yourself at a loss for words when a friend or family member needs encouragement? Our context today is the third of the great Servant songs of Isaiah that are ultimately fulfilled only in Christ. This song speaks of the Servant's understanding of the active fury of those who despise Him. He speaks of giving His back to those who strike him and refusing to cover His face from humiliation and spitting (v. 6). How does one face such hostility without becoming discouraged? The answer will challenge and inform you.

On four occasions the Servant begins a declaration with the phrase, "The Lord God" (vv. 4, 5, 7, 9). This phrase could be translated as "Sovereign God" or "My Master, God." In other words, the Servant declares His absolute submission to God, which is where He finds His necessary help. In verses 4 and 5, He indicates what the Lord has given Him, and in verses 7 and 9, He affirms the Lord's help.

What did the Lord give Him that provided such assistance? He gave Him the tongue of disciples and opened His ear. The phrase "tongue of disciples" is a curious one, but it simply means the tongue of one who has been instructed in speaking the word of God. The Servant learned through His own rejection how to comfort others who were weary and discouraged.

The Servant gives us several important principles we can use to develop an "instructed tongue." First, He gave regular and consistent attention to the instruction of the Lord. "He awakens Me morning by morning, He awakens My ear to listen as a disciple." (v. 4). Second, He was obedient to all that God taught Him (v. 5). Finally, this obedience confirmed His trust in the Lord. "Let him trust in the name of the Lord and rely on his God" (v. 10).

Do you start each day with God's Word? Do you submit to Him in total obedience? This is the path to personal trust—the only path that will enable you to strengthen others as well.

GOD HAS
SHOWN US WONDERS

> **Daniel 4:2** It has seemed good to me to declare the signs and wonders which the Most High God has done for me.

This verse contains a most unusual declaration, for it comes from the mouth of Nebuchadnezzar, the king of Babylon. He begins by praising God for His signs and wonders and declares that His kingdom is an everlasting kingdom.

You may be familiar with the story line of the book of Daniel. God's people had been taken into captivity, and King Nebuchadnezzar conducted an experiment by bringing some of the Israelite youth into his court for training. Four of these youth had a tremendous impact on the king and his country. Even though these young people were placed in a pagan environment, they were unwilling to compromise their convictions about the one true God and His requirements for them. Through all the testing they proved themselves to be ten times better than the conjurers and magicians of the land (1:20).

These young people were instrumental in the spiritual awakening that occurred in the life of Nebuchadnezzar. First, Daniel was able to interpret a dream for the king that none of his wise men could reconstruct or comprehend. Next, when the three Israelites were cast into the fiery furnace for refusing to worship a golden image, God delivered them unharmed.

These clear evidences of God's miraculous intervention led the king to make a decree that no one could say anything offensive about the one true God (3:29). Daniel recorded the story in Nebuchadnezzar's own words. The king begins by saying that "it has seemed good" or "it is my pleasure" to declare what God has done.

This should be the attitude of each of us. We should be thrilled with any and every opportunity to tell what God has done for us. The testimony of Nebuchadnezzar is both eloquent and accurate—"How great are His signs and how mighty are His wonders! His kingdom is an everlasting kingdom and His dominion is from generation to generation" (4:3). May this be our declaration as well.

GOD HAS
Delivered Us

> **Daniel 6:20** Daniel, servant of the living God, has your God, whom you constantly serve, been able to deliver you from the lions?

No doubt you have already discovered that conviction is often costly. When we choose to live by our convictions, it will sometimes cause others to ridicule or even persecute us. Is it worth it? Ask Daniel!

Because of the favor of God, Daniel was promoted by King Darius to a leading political office in Babylon. He began to distinguish himself from other officers "because he possessed an extraordinary spirit" (v. 3). The king decided to appoint him over the entire kingdom. The other officers were jealous and tried to find some way to accuse Daniel of corruption. But Daniel was a man of such character and conviction, they knew their only hope was to create a situation where he would be required to do something contrary to the law of God (v. 5).

A plan was devised. The officers convinced the king to enforce an injunction that anyone making a petition to any god or man besides the king would be cast into the lions' den. As soon as the petition was signed, Daniel entered his house, opened his window, and knelt to pray. The king had no recourse but to enforce his own foolish law, and thus Daniel was thrown into the den of lions.

The king spent the night fasting. Then at dawn he rushed to the lions' den. The "God Has" promise is contained in the king's question. Notice that the focus is on God and Daniel, a man who "constantly" serves Him. Daniel's service was not one of convenience but conviction. The fact that the king called out to Daniel indicates he already suspected the answer.

But to quell the king's fear, Daniel declared that God had sent an angel to protect him since he was innocent (v. 22). Daniel was removed from the lions' den without injury "because he had trusted in his God." (v. 23). God's deliverance can take many forms. But when we live by conviction, we can be assured of His protection and deliverance.

GOD HAS
JOINED US TOGETHER

> **Matthew 19:6** So they are no longer two, but one flesh. What therefore God has joined together, let no man separate.

What constitutes marriage and family has become a hot political issue. Do we have the right to define marriage as we choose, or is there a divine pattern that should not be ignored?

The nation of Israel was divided over the issue of marriage and divorce. Followers of Rabbi Hillel felt that a man could divorce his wife for nearly any reason. Others who followed Shammai argued for divorce only on the grounds of a sexual offense. The context suggests that the Pharisees, who asked Jesus the question concerning divorce, were more interested in testing Jesus (v. 3) than hearing His answer. If He sided with one of the popular teachers, He would alienate a large percentage of those who gathered to hear Him.

Rather than getting involved in the controversy, Jesus reminded them of God's original purpose for establishing the marriage bond. He then quoted Genesis 1:27, where God established marriage as the permanent union between a man and a woman, creating a bond which takes precedence over one's commitment to parents. He then added the words that have become commonplace in virtually every religious wedding ceremony.

Jesus spoke of this new relationship as having such intimacy that the two become one flesh. He further indicated that this union is a miraculous activity of God who has joined the man and woman together. Tragically the Pharisees missed Jesus' point about the miracle of marriage and wanted to pit Him against Moses, who allowed for a certificate of divorce. Jesus' response that the "divorce provision" was because of "your hardness of heart" (v. 8) and was intended as an indictment of the Pharisees who would rather argue the details of the law than celebrate the activity of God.

God loves us so much that He cares about all our relationships. Whether the ceremony is civil or religious, only God can join two persons, creating one flesh.

GOD HAS
DONE GREAT THINGS

> **Luke 8:39** Return to your house and describe what great things God has done for you.

Some studies indicate that only about five percent of believers have ever told anyone about their personal relationship with Christ. If this number is even close to accurate, it is one of the greatest tragedies of our day. Perhaps we have inadvertently made witnessing too difficult, suggesting that significant training is required to be an effective witness.

Jesus had been approached by a man who was living among the tombs because he had been possessed by a legion of demons. Jesus cast the demons out of the man and into a herd of swine. The herdsmen then rushed into town to tell about the recent events, and a crowd quickly gathered to find that the demonic man sitting at the feet of Jesus was fully clothed and in his right mind.

We are stunned to discover that the people wanted Jesus to leave. Luke tells us they were gripped with fear. Unbelievers do not necessarily turn to God even when they witness His mighty power. But while the villagers wanted Jesus to leave, the former demoniac wanted to join Him. In fact, he begged Jesus to let him accompany Him.

Jesus, however, instructed the man to return home and describe the "great things" God had done for him. The man had been forced from his home because of his demonic condition, and now he was commanded to go back as a witness to the power of God. His response was immediate and complete: "He went away, proclaiming throughout the whole city what great things Jesus had done for him."

God would not leave this city without a witness. Even though they had rejected Jesus out of fear, they would now be confronted daily with a visible and audible reminder of the great things God had done.

What great things has God done for you? You are a witness to these things where you live. Have you told anyone lately about the great things God has done? Why not tell someone today?

GOD HAS
Set His Seal

> **John 6:27** For on Him the
> Father, God, has set His seal.

Have you ever had a document nota-
rized? If so, you understand the purpose of
a seal. The seal of a notary signifies that the
document is authentic.

John indicated that a large crowd
followed Jesus because they saw the signs
He was performing as He healed the sick
(v. 2). Seeing the multitude that had
gathered, Jesus instructed His disciples to
seat the people. He then fed the crowd of
five thousand with five barley loaves and
two fish He borrowed from a young lad.

After dark, Jesus and His disciples
crossed the lake to Capernaum—they in a
boat, and He on the sea. Discovering that
Jesus was missing, the people got into their
boats and went to find Him. Jesus confronted them with a sad truth: "Truly, truly,
I say to you, you seek Me, not because you
saw signs, but because you ate of the loaves
and were filled" (v. 26). The miracles of

Jesus were "signs" given to point men beyond the event itself to the one who worked the miracle. The people had been driven more by physical appetite than by spiritual need.

Jesus seized upon this teachable moment to help the crowd prioritize the spiritual over the temporal. Physical food satisfies one's hunger for only a moment. Jesus offered them a food which endures to eternal life. Later in this same conversation, Jesus made it clear He was talking about Himself. "I am the bread of life; he who comes to Me will not hunger, and he who believes in Me will never thirst" (v. 35).

But how could they believe such a wonderful promise? Here's why: God had set His seal on Jesus, thus authenticating Him as the one true King! The Father had done this before at Jesus' baptism when He declared, "This is My beloved Son" (Matt. 3:17). Yet the most convincing truth was when the Father raised Him from the dead (see Rom. 1:4). Yes, you can trust in Jesus. The Father has set His seal on Him.

GOD HAS
GIVEN HIS HOLY SPIRIT

> **Acts 5:32** We are witnesses of these things; and so is the Holy Spirit, whom God has given to those who obey Him.

God has given all believers a gift that enables them to effectively serve Him and live victoriously. This gift is His Holy Spirit who indwells and empowers us.

The early apostles were hauled before the highest court of the Jews for proclaiming the resurrection of the dead (4:2). When asked by what power or in whose name they had acted, Peter told them they were acting in the name of Jesus Christ the Nazarene (v. 10). The members of the Sanhedrin could not deny the miraculous works being accomplished, nor could they afford to let this message of the resurrection spread further. So they threatened the disciples, commanding them not to speak any longer in Jesus' name (v. 17).

The disciples were undeterred by the threat and continued to preach and do mighty works in the name of Jesus. The high priest and the Sadducees were filled with jealousy and threw the apostles into jail (5:17). But they were released by an angel who commanded them to teach in the temple. When the high priest and his associates were informed that the prisoners were out preaching, they had them seized.

The high priest reminded them that they had been given strict orders not to continue teaching in this name (v. 28). Peter and the apostles answered that they must obey God rather than man. Once again they declared to the council the truth of the crucifixion, resurrection, and exaltation of Christ who alone can provide forgiveness of sins (v. 31).

Not only were the apostles witnesses of these things, but their testimony had been corroborated by the Holy Spirit. He was the one who had produced their miraculous signs and powerful preaching. God gave them the Holy Spirit as a consequence of their belief in God's Son for redemption. And this same Spirit is given to all who believe in Christ (Rom. 8:9). If you have received Christ as your Savior, the Holy Spirit lives in you and will give you boldness to declare the good news.

GOD HAS
GRANTED REPENTANCE

> **Acts 11:18** God has granted
> to the Gentiles also the
> repentance that leads to life.

The word "repentance" may not be one of our favorite words. It assumes we have sinned and therefore have something for which we need to repent. But this "God Has" promise ends with great news— "repentance that leads to life."

Cornelius, a Gentile, had a vision which led him to invite Simon Peter to visit him in Caesarea. Peter, a Jew by birth, had been taught that it was unlawful for a Jew to associate or visit with a foreigner (10:28). Yet God had prepared Peter for this moment by giving him a dream which taught him that he should not call any man unclean.

Peter preached to them the incredible news that all persons of every nation who fear God and do what is right can become acceptable to God (v. 35). He then declared the realities concerning the life, death, and resurrection of Jesus, concluding that the prophets agree that "through His name everyone who believes in Him receives forgiveness of sins" (v. 43).

Before Peter finished preaching, the gift of the Holy Spirit was poured out upon the Gentiles who had gathered to hear what Peter had to say. Peter, seeing the evidence of the Spirit, ordered them to be baptized in the name of Jesus Christ.

Word of this event spread throughout Judea. When Peter returned to Jerusalem, some of the brethren were upset that Peter went to the uncircumcised and ate with them (11:2-3). Peter recounted the entire story, concluding that if God gave them the gift of the Spirit in the same way the Jews had received the Spirit, he could not stand in God's way (v. 17). Peter's testimony led to a celebration as they glorified God for granting to the Gentiles repentance that leads to life.

I frequently encounter people who are sorry for their sin, but their sorrow has only led to regret and despair. The only solution for sin is to repent or turn from our sin and turn to God, who through Christ forgives our sin and gives us life.

GOD HAS
BROUGHT US A SAVIOR

> **Acts 13:23** From the descendants of this man, according to promise, God has brought to Israel a Savior, Jesus.

We sometimes use the word "savior" with glib familiarity. We may refer to someone who arrived just in the nick of time to bail us out of an embarrassing situation as having "saved our life." We may speak of a military hero as one who saved our country. Paul, however, is not talking about a hero who rescues us in this life, but one who has the power to forgive sin and make us right with God.

Paul was on his first missionary journey, speaking to "men of Israel and you who fear God" (v. 16). Those "who fear God" is a reference to Gentiles who worshipped the God of Israel but had not yet become full-fledged converts.

Paul began with a brief survey of Israel's history, including the stay in Egypt, the forty year sojourn in the wilderness, the conquest of the land, the period of the judges, the rule of Samuel, and the desire for a king. Reading the entire context, you will notice that the pace of history dramatically slows with the mention of David.

David is described as a man after God's heart. But Paul's real interest was in the promise made to David. In 2 Samuel 7:12–16 we find the promise that one whose kingdom will last forever will come from David's lineage. Paul declared that this promise has been fulfilled.

He picked up the narrative with the coming of John the Baptist, who preached a baptism of repentance to prepare people for the Savior. Then Paul delivered the punch line: "Brethren, sons of Abraham's family, and those among you who fear God, to us the message of this salvation has been sent" (v. 26).

After this, Paul surveyed the rejection, crucifixion, and resurrection of Jesus, demonstrating that Jesus alone was qualified to fulfill all the promises of God concerning a King with an eternal kingdom. He ended with a triumphant note we must heed today: "Through Him forgiveness of sins is proclaimed to you" (13:38). Do you know Jesus as your Savior?

GOD HAS
GIVEN FAITH TO ALL

> **Romans 12:3 (NIV)** Think of yourself
> with sober judgment, in accordance with
> the measure of faith God has given you.

As a child, were you ever the last one
selected when your class was choosing up
sides for a game during recess? If so, you
know it makes you feel left out. I have
discovered that many Christians fail to
serve God through their church because
they believe they have been left out when it
comes to being gifted for service. Ever feel
that way? This promise is for you.

Paul calls upon believers to present their
bodies to God as a living and holy sacrifice. He not only indicates that this is our
"spiritual service of worship" (v. 1) but tells
us that such a gift has already been deemed
"acceptable." It is encouraging to know that
we have an offering to give the King which
He desires and declares "acceptable."

In order to make such an offering, we
must be transformed by the renewing of
the mind (v. 2). We have two options: we
can be conformed to the thinking of the

world, or we can be transformed by allowing the Spirit to renew our mind. This means we will begin to view ourselves from God's vantage point rather than from the world's perspective. This, Paul indicates, will allow us to know and do (to "prove") the will of God, which is good, acceptable, and perfect.

Paul then calls us to sound judgment based upon an essential truth: "God has allotted to each a measure of faith." This phrase must be interpreted by the ensuing discussion concerning how each member of the body functions properly. This only happens when each member utilizes the unique gifts they have been given (vv. 6–8). He mentions abilities such as prophecy, service, teaching, exhortation, giving, leading, and showing mercy. These gifts, along with others mentioned in 1 Corinthians 12, are not comprehensive in nature, but show the sorts of ability one could use in serving the King.

When Paul says God has allotted you a measure of faith, he is speaking of the supernatural ability to serve the King acceptably. Are you doing that?

GOD HAS
ACCEPTED US

> **Romans 14:3** The one who does not eat is not to judge the one who eats, for God has accepted him.

We might as well come clean. We all struggle with judging other believers. It might be as simple as their diet, as is the case in this passage, or it might be something we consider to be more substantial, like dress or musical preference. Whatever the issue, we can learn from this text not to judge others.

Paul advised the believers in Rome to accept into their fellowship a person "who is weak in faith, but not for the purpose of passing judgment on his opinions" (v. 1). It would be less than genuine to accept one as a brother and then commence to pass judgment on the person's opinions. The word "opinion" suggests an issue that might well be disputed among believers. In other words, it is not an issue of primary theological significance.

The issue in Rome was one of diet. Some of the people were of the opinion that they could eat anything they wanted, while others were vegetarians (v. 2). Because some of the meat sold in the marketplace had been offered to idols (see 1 Cor. 8), it is possible that the vegetarians were scrupulously avoiding all meat to avoid any compromise with pagan practices.

Whatever the reason for the difference of opinion, Paul's counsel was that they must not regard the other with contempt. We all have a tendency to ridicule a lifestyle that is more or less restrictive than our own. Such an attitude reflects our arrogance in assuming that our opinion is the correct one. It takes humility of spirit to live in community.

The key phrase that should keep us from looking down on Christian brothers and sisters who are different is the reminder that "God has accepted him." If God has accepted him, what right do we have to judge his opinions? Paul addresses this in verse 4. "To his own master he stands or falls; and he will stand, for the Lord is able to make him stand." Aren't we glad that God has accepted us and can make us stand in spite of all our failings?

GOD HAS
CHOSEN THE WEAK

> **1 Corinthians 1:27** God has chosen the weak things of the world to shame the things which are strong.

Have you ever watched a child choose a toy or a piece of candy? They allow their hand to pause over each item as they carefully weigh their options. Most often they will select either the largest piece of candy or the shiniest toy replete with bells and whistles. As a mature adult you may try to advise your children to choose based on quality, but the world's standards say to choose the largest and shiniest. If you don't feel you have much of value to offer the Lord, you will be thrilled to learn that God chooses that which the world often rejects.

Some of the Corinthians arrogantly boasted about their gifts and wisdom, their leaders and freedom. Paul corrected their self-evaluation by pointing first to the message he preached: "Christ crucified" (v. 23). This message was a stumbling block to the Jews and foolishness to the Gentiles. Who could imagine a king who was crucified? Yet "the foolishness of God is wiser than men, and the weakness of God is stronger than men" (v. 25).

Second, he suggested they take an internal audit of their own congregation. From a human perspective they came up short when measured by the world's standards of power, nobility, wisdom, and influence. God has turned the world's standards upside down. He has chosen people whom the world might view as weak or foolish so that He alone will receive the glory.

Don't miss the point of this kingdom promise: "God has chosen you!" If you're like me, this point is too wonderful to comprehend. Paul elaborates, "But by His doing you are in Christ Jesus, who became to us wisdom from God, and righteousness and sanctification, and redemption" (v. 30). Everything the world strives for has been made available to us in Christ Jesus.

This sobering but incredible truth leads to an obvious conclusion: "Let him who boasts, boast in the Lord" (v. 31). God has chosen you and placed you in Christ, enabling you to serve Him effectively.

GOD HAS
PREPARED RICH BLESSINGS

{ **1 Corinthians 2:9 (NIV)** No eye has
seen, no ear has heard, no mind has
conceived what God has prepared
for those who love him. }

Have you ever been given a gift that
was simply overwhelming? You are so
taken by the generosity of the gift that you
can hardly believe your own eyes. This
promise indicates that God has prepared
rich blessings for those who love Him
which exceed all we have seen or heard.

To understand this kingdom promise we
must give attention to its context. Some
persons in Corinth had found Paul's
teaching to lack superiority of speech and
wisdom (v. 2). Paul agreed that his message was delivered in weakness, fear, and
trembling because the power of his message was not based on his fleshly strength
and persuasiveness but on the demonstration of the power of the Spirit (v. 4).

Further, Paul indicated that his message
contained wisdom for the mature. It was a
wisdom the rulers of this age rejected (v.
6). God's wisdom is the mystery of salva-

tion through a crucified Messiah. The irony is that when the rulers of this age rejected this wisdom by crucifying Christ, they unwittingly carried out God's prior will, "predestined before the ages to our glory" (vv. 8–9). Why were the rulers blinded to this wisdom? It was "hidden by and in God" and could only be revealed through the Spirit (v. 10).

Paul fortifies this great truth by quoting an amalgamation of Old Testament texts, loosely based on Isaiah 64:4 and 65:16. First, he concludes that men, unaided by the Spirit, cannot conceive the bounteous blessing God has prepared for them. Second, they are ignorant of the redemption made available in Christ which releases these blessings in the lives of those who love God. But the believer can know them because they are revealed through the Spirit, who is from God (vv. 10–12).

Have you asked God to show you His blessings? Have you spent time in prayer and the study of His Word to mine those riches? "We have received . . . the Spirit who is from God, so that we may know the things freely given to us by God" (v. 12).

GOD HAS
RAISED HIS SON

> **1 Corinthians 6:14** God has not only raised the Lord, but will also raise us up through His power.

The most significant event in all of human history is the resurrection of Jesus Christ. While we affirm this truth, we sometimes forget that biblical events occurred in the context of world history and, as such, impact every area of our lives.

Once again it is important for us to look at the context in which this great affirmation occurs. Paul is dealing with the matter of Christian liberty which had been taken to an extreme by some in Corinth. Verse 12 probably reflects a slogan of those with a libertine view, along with Paul's corrective. "All things are lawful for me, but not all things are profitable. All things are lawful for me, but I will not be mastered by anything."

He then spoke specifically to the issue of food and the stomach (v. 13). Some in Corinth arrogantly ate food that had been offered to pagan idols. They claimed the idol had no meaning, and their freedom gave them the right to do so. They had little concern about their witness. He also spoke of sexual immorality. Apparently some of the believers saw no problem with their Christian commitment and sexual promiscuity.

You may be wondering what an affirmation about the resurrection has to do with how we use our physical body. The answer is—"everything." Notice that Paul not only affirms that God has raised Jesus from the dead, but he also indicates that God will raise us up through His power. This means that our redemption has implications for the physical as well as the spiritual.

"Yet the body is not for immorality, but for the Lord, and the Lord is for the body" is the statement that precedes the affirmation that God has raised Jesus. Later Paul would declare that since we are one spirit with the Lord, our body is a temple of the Holy Spirit (v.19).

Does your lifestyle reflect that you have been raised up with Christ? In what ways can you glorify God in your body?

GOD HAS
PLACED US IN HIS BODY

> **1 Corinthians 12:18** God has
> placed the members, each
> one of them, in the body,
> just as He desired.

Have you ever felt left out or unappreci-
ated? Do you sometimes think your life has
little meaning and that you have little
impact on the world? I have a great kingdom promise just for you. You were
created by God, redeemed by His grace,
gifted by His Spirit, and placed in His
body by His specific desire!

As you read 1 Corinthians, it becomes
clear that some members of this community
were quite proud of their spiritual gifts and
sought every opportunity to display those
gifts in a manner that brought attention to
themselves. This arrogant display of a few
spectacular gifts had led others to conclude
that they themselves were not as gifted and
thus were of little value to the church.

Paul refuted both the arrogance of some
and the under evaluation of others by
arguing that all true believers are recipients
of the Spirit and thus all are gifted for

service to the King. He used the analogy of the human body to illustrate the necessity of different gifts. The ear, for example, should not conclude that it is unimportant to the body simply because it does not function as the eye does (v. 16). After all, what would the body be like if every member functioned as an eye (v. 17)?

The bottom line is that each member has a unique function because it has been placed into the body by the specific design and desire of the Creator. In case you are thinking this truth does not apply to you, notice the statement "each one of them." If you sometimes feel you are insignificant, you should keep reading. Paul argues that those members who "seem to be weaker" are necessary (v. 22). In fact, he concludes that "God has so composed the body, giving more abundant honor to that member which lacked" (v. 24).

You are special to God! He designed you with His church in mind so that you could join with other gifted members to advance His kingdom, by His power, and for His glory.

GOD HAS
APPOINTED LEADERS

> **1 Corinthians 12:28** God has appointed in the church, first apostles, second prophets, third teachers, then miracles.

Once in a while we all have a tendency to rebel against authority and structure. Something about that "don't walk on the grass" sign makes us want to take a stroll there. Yet we know that life would be chaotic if there weren't structure and persons in authority. Believe it or not, God has appointed leaders in the church to enable it to function effectively.

Some of the members in Corinth who were proud of their powerful gifts paraded them in the assembly with little concern for the edification of the body. They saw their gifts as a sign of their advanced spirituality, not as evidence of God's grace enabling them to edify others in the congregation. This arrogance had led to factions based on the various leaders who had served in Corinth. Some saw Paul and other apostles as being rather weak when it came to gifts and wisdom (4:6–13).

This kingdom promise is found just a few verses below the one we looked at in our previous discussion. After asserting that God has composed the body as He desired, giving more honor to those that are often viewed as unseemly, Paul concludes with this listing of gifted members that God has appointed in the church.

It is not insignificant that he lists apostles, prophets, and teachers first with a numerical reference. Since some in Corinth were so assured of their own spirituality that they saw no need for leaders, Paul wanted them to understand that God appoints leaders just as he appoints those who manifest miracles or gifts of healings. It is also worthy of note, as you read in the latter part of the verse, that Paul includes helps and administrations—rather mundane abilities. This list was intended to expand the understanding of many in Corinth who tended to see leaders and administrators as a necessary nuisance.

Isn't it wonderful that God has composed the body for effective ministry, providing everyone necessary to enable the church to advance the kingdom?

GOD HAS
SENT FORTH HIS SPIRIT

> **Galatians 4:6** Because you
> are sons, God has sent forth
> the Spirit of His Son into our
> hearts, crying, "Abba! Father!"

Nothing is quite as moving as a son or daughter tenderly calling out to their father. Whether spoken at the father's return from a long business trip or when he arrives home after a day's work, nothing refreshes the soul more than the word "father."

In the Galatian letter, Paul wrote of the privilege of "sonship" and the role of the Spirit in the work of redemption—how a person becomes a son or daughter of God. Paul spoke of the days when the Galatians were in bondage under the elemental things of the world. But when the time was right, God sent His Son to redeem man, who was unable to live up to the lofty standards of the law by human will alone.

He speaks here of redemption in terms of adoption. There is no contradiction between the image of new birth and adoption. Adoption may be intended to place a stronger emphasis on God's personal choice to make each believer His child. The evidence that we are now sons is the indwelling presence of the Holy Spirit. The term "Spirit of His Son" is used in this context to underline the theme of sonship of all believers.

Isn't it wonderful that our sonship is the basis for receiving the Spirit, and that the gift of the Spirit is the means through which we become conscious of our personal relationship to the Father? In other words, the Spirit grants us new life and then assures us of the reality of that life. Thus Paul declares that, in contrast to the law which is an external authority, the Spirit is sent to renew our hearts and convince us inwardly of the truth of His presence.

It is this conviction that prompts us to cry out "Abba! Father!" This passionate, personal cry is the joy of redemption (see Rom. 8:15). It hearkens back to the promise of the Lord's Prayer, where Jesus taught His followers to address the omnipotent God as "our Father." Have you experienced the personal redemption through the Spirit that allows you to call God your Father?

GOD HAS
SANCTIFIED US

> **1 Thessalonians 4:7** God has not called us for the purpose of impurity, but in sanctification.

We live in a culture inundated by sexual images and exploitation. So-called "family" programs are no longer safe for children to watch unsupervised. Sex is used to sell virtually every product. It is the punch line of most humor in our world today. How does the Christian live in a culture so permeated by sexual promiscuity?

Paul addressed this matter in a clear manner in verses 3–8 of 1 Thessalonians 4. He begins with a simple statement of fact: "For this is the will of God, your sanctification; that is, that you abstain from sexual immorality" (v. 3). I often hear Christians say they want to know how to discern the will of God for their lives. I know they are referring to issues such as their profession or potential spouse. I can tell you with absolute assurance one thing you can know for certain about the will of God—His desire that you remain sexually pure.

Living by lustful passion describes pagans who do not know God. Persons without a personal knowledge of God do not have the power of the Holy Spirit to keep lustful passions in check and thus often act out of selfish desire (vv. 4–5). It is clear that God is not against sexual expression. He created us male and female and provided for us the joy of sexual intimacy within marriage. Thus the Christian is to "possess his own vessel in sanctification and honor" (v. 4). Believers do not look upon their spouse as a tool to satisfy physical lust, but as a part of one's own flesh and a member of God's holy people.

Paul affirms that God has called us in sanctification. The emphasis on God's calling underlines both His power and the new order of life for the one who is called. The believer is "called" to sanctification. Just as impurity once characterized our experience, now purity characterizes those who have been called. The ability to overcome sexual passion is provided by the Holy Spirit who has been given (v. 8).

GOD HAS
DESTINED US FOR SALVATION

> **1 Thessalonians 5:9** God has
> not destined us for wrath, but
> for obtaining salvation through
> our Lord Jesus Christ.

My oldest daughter once shared the gospel with a college classmate. Afterward her classmate said that the implications of what Tina had proposed meant that those who rejected the gospel would spend eternity in hell. When Tina agreed, the friend responded that she could never serve a God who would send someone to hell. My daughter wisely responded that God loves us so much that He went there Himself in the person of His Son so that no one would have to suffer that fate.

This particular "God Has" promise begins with a negative assertion, then follows it with the positive. God has not destined us for wrath. God created man in His own image so that we could have fellowship with Him while on earth and then dwell with Him in heaven for all eternity. He has not only destined us for salvation, but He also has provided the means of that salvation through His own Son, the Lord Jesus Christ.

Salvation and its eternal consequences are not issues of vague hope, nor is salvation something we must seek to earn on our own merits. The way was costly. Verse 10 indicates that our Lord Jesus Christ "died for us, so that whether we are awake or asleep, we will live together with Him." Christ, who knew no sin, died in our place, paying the penalty for our sin so that we might live with Him. The words "awake or asleep" refer to life and death. The context of this promise is the return of our Lord. Paul assures believers that whether they die before Christ's return or live until His return, they will dwell with Him forever.

Talk about stress relief! Knowing where you will spend eternity is the ultimate relaxation therapy. Paul repeats this promise in 2 Thessalonians 2:13 with a weightier explanation—"God has chosen you from the beginning for salvation through sanctification by the Spirit and faith in the truth." Have you put your faith in the truth of the gospel? Check out the last few pages of this book to make sure.

GOD HAS
GIVEN US POWER

> **2 Timothy 2:7** God has not
> given us a spirit of timidity,
> but of power and love
> and discipline.

Do you ever feel afraid? What frightens
you the most? Is it the thought of war or
the fear of a global economic panic? Is
your fear a more personal issue? Matters
such as job security, public speaking,
personal relationships, and health can all
cause us to respond with fear and timidity.

The letters to Timothy are personal and
pastoral correspondence from the aging
apostle Paul to the one he called his "beloved son" (v. 2). He exhorted Timothy to
"kindle afresh" the gift of God within him
(v. 6), not inferring that Timothy's zeal was
flagging, but reminding him that one's faith
must always be stirred to full flame.

Paul begins verse 7 with a negative
assertion in order to lay a foundation for
the threefold gift of God: "power and love
and discipline."

"Power" is the supernatural ability to
live the Christian life successfully and to

accomplish God's purposes. We need to remind ourselves that the Christian life must always be lived by the power of the Holy Spirit. If you are ever tempted to think you can produce the fruit of Christian living through an exertion of self-will, just listen to Jesus: "Truly, truly, I say to you, the Son can do nothing of Himself" (John 5:19).

"Love" describes both the focus and the goal of power. Love enables us to endure the most difficult and challenging circumstances. We are reminded of Paul's testimony to the Corinthians—how love "bears all things, believes all things, hopes all things, endures all things; love never fails" (1 Cor. 13:7–8).

"Discipline" is the structure in which power and love function. Discipline describes a life of balance. If you are tempted to argue that you are not the disciplined type, you need to remember that discipline itself is a gift of God.

Here's the bottom line: God has gifted you with the resources for every circumstance and situation. Thus you can face life with confidence and not timidity.

GOD HAS
SENT HIS SON

{ **1 John 4:9** God has sent His only begotten Son into the world so that we might live through Him. }

As I mature, people regularly tell me that I look more like my father every day. I take this as a compliment, admitting that I do see "Daddy's genes" becoming more apparent in me. I pray that people can see my heavenly Father's genes becoming more dominant in my life as I mature spiritually.

John, in his first epistle, placed a strong emphasis on love. On numerous occasions he exhorted believers to love one another. But John was not making a mere expression of affection; he was calling believers to love one another in the same manner that God has loved us.

John declares that "God is love" (v. 8). God does not love because the object of His love is worthy of it; He loves because it is His very nature to do so. His love is not an emotional feeling but an active expression—and a costly one. See how the thought of verse 9 is repeated again in verse 10—"He loved us and sent His Son to be the propitiation for our sins." The supreme manifestation of God's love was the sending of His only begotten Son to pay the penalty for our sin.

This self-giving, undeserved love is the kind to which we are called as believers. I know you must be thinking that such a depth of love is beyond your natural ability. You're right. But you may be missing a key component of this passage. The first part of verse 9 says that the love of God is "manifested in us." God did not simply display His love to us by sending His Son; He made us new creatures capable of manifesting His love to others. You might say love is in our new DNA. We are the children of the Father, whose character is love.

This is why John could boldly assert that everyone who loves is born of God and knows God; conversely, the one who does *not* love does *not* know God (vv. 7–8). Our ability to love others is not dependent on our own ability, but upon the abiding Holy Spirit (v. 13) who manifests the character of God in us. Anyone accused you of looking like your Dad lately?

GOD HAS
GIVEN US ETERNAL LIFE

> **1 John 5:11** The testimony is
> this, that God has given
> us eternal life, and this
> life is in His Son.

Have you heard the joke that only two
things are certain—death and taxes?
Everyone chuckles, even though they
know the punch line. But death is no
laughing matter! Since death is certain, it is
critical that we know what will occur the
moment we die. Are you certain you will
have eternal life? Will you spend eternity
in the presence of your Creator?

This was John's solitary purpose for
writing his first letter. "These things I have
written to you who believe in the name of
the Son of God, so that you may know that
you have eternal life" (v. 13).

What evidence does John bring to the
table to assure us we have eternal life? Did
you notice that our promise begins with the
mention of "testimony"? If we are trying to
establish the truth of a matter, we gather
corroborating evidence. John speaks of
three witnesses: "the Spirit and the water

and the blood" (v. 8). He indicates further that the three witnesses are in agreement.

The Holy Spirit can be trusted because He is the "Spirit of truth" (John 14:17). Do you remember what Jesus told His disciples at the point of His departure? "But when He, the Spirit of truth, comes, He will guide you into all the truth; for He will not speak on His own initiative, but whatever He hears, He will speak" (John 16:13). The Holy Spirit speaks truth revealed by the Father.

"Water and the blood" refer to the baptism and crucifixion of Jesus, the bookends of His ministry. At His baptism the Father testified, "You are My beloved Son, in You I am well-pleased" (Mark 1:11). Jesus' willingness to be obedient to the point of death was the ultimate testimony to the truth of His claim to be God's Son and to give eternal life. Deuteronomy 19:15 stresses the need of three witnesses in agreement to confirm a matter. Thus we have confirmation!

Because of this testimony, we can know that the one who believes in Christ has eternal life. Do you know?

GOD HAS
GIVEN US UNDERSTANDING

> **1 John 5:20** We know that the Son of God has come, and has given us understanding so that we may know Him who is true.

Confidence is an important component to our success in virtually any endeavor. In sports, confidence gives us a mental edge as we enter competition. When we interview for a job, make a business presentation, teach a Sunday school class, or sing a solo, we prepare so that we are confident when we speak, teach, or sing. Our knowledge of the material is a critical component of building confidence.

This final section of John's letter begins with an assertion that John has written these materials "so that you may know that you have eternal life" (v. 13). The knowledge provided by the inspired writings of John not only leads us to Christ, but it also gives us "confidence" before the Father when we pray (vv. 14–15). In this kingdom promise we will focus our attention on the final powerful "we know" in this first letter of John.

Believers can boldly affirm that "we know that the Son of God has come." The coming of the Son "has given us understanding." The term translated "understanding" occurs only here in John's writings. It speaks of insight which leads to personal perception. What has this "understanding" allowed us to know for certain? We know "Him who is true." Notice the rapid-fire, three-fold repetition of the word "true" toward the end of verse 20, culminating in the declaration — "This is the true God and eternal life."

It is important to note that the promise of understanding is not followed by a subjective understanding of truth in general. The object of our understanding is a person. God is truth, which means that He alone is ultimate reality. How did we come to understand that He alone is truth? God communicated this by sending His own Son. When you understand that God alone is the true God, it means that all other gods are "idols" (v. 21). We are protected from them by truth.

Do you know the one true God? He is comprehended only in Christ.

GOD HAS
ILLUMINED HIS CITY

> **Revelation 21:23** The city has no
> need of the sun or of the moon to
> shine on it, for the glory of God has
> illumined it, and its lamp is the Lamb.

Do you think about heaven very often?
Sometimes when I am flying and I look out
of the windows at the billowy clouds and
the earth beneath, I think of what heaven
might be like. Both my mom and dad are
there, and I think about what they might
be doing in heaven. Through the years I
have noticed that the older I get, the more I
think about heaven.

John, in the book we call Revelation,
gives us a few glimpses into the heavenly
city. You must understand that John was
limited by his earthly vocabulary as he
attempted to describe the incredible beauty
of our heavenly home.

We may be awed by the description of a
city whose brilliance was like "crystal-clear
jasper" (v. 11). We are impressed by the
massive, high wall with twelve gates
attended by twelve angels (vv. 12–13). The
foundation stones arrest our attention since

they are adorned with "every kind of precious stone" (vv. 19–20). The street of pure gold has inspired musicians of every age (v. 21).

But all of these descriptions pale in comparison to the presence of Almighty God. The city, modeled after the Holy of Holies, has no need for a temple because all is holy and God is everywhere adored. The sun and moon cease to exist since their splendor and radiance has been surpassed by the glory of God Himself. Our final kingdom promise assures us that "God has illumined it." Heaven is glorious and bright because its very illumination is God. The vessel through whom God provides illumination is the Lamb. Can you imagine what it will be like to live eternally in the presence of Him who is perfect light?

By the way, we won't be alone. "The nations will walk by its light and the kings of the earth will bring their glory into it" (v. 24). You may wonder who will be present among them—"Only those whose names are written in the Lamb's book of life" (v. 27). To be certain yours is written there, turn the page and follow God's instruction.

APPENDIX

The promises of this book are based on one's relationship to Christ. If you have not yet entered a personal relationship with Jesus Christ, I encourage you to make this wonderful discovery today. I like to use the very simple acrostic—LIFE—to explain this, knowing that God wants you not only to inherit *eternal* life but also to experience *earthly* life to its fullest.

L = LOVE

It all begins with God's love. God created you in his image. This means you were created to live in relationship with him. *"For God loved the world in this way: He gave His One and Only Son, so that everyone who believes in Him will not perish but have eternal life"* (John 3:16).

But if God loves you and desires a relationship with you, why do you feel so isolated from him?

I = ISOLATION

This isolation is created by our sin—our rebellion against God—which separates us from him and from others. *"For all have sinned and fall short of the glory of God"* (Rom. 3:23). *"For the wages of sin is death, but the gift of God is eternal life in Christ Jesus our Lord"* (Rom. 6:23).

You might wonder how you can overcome this isolation and have an intimate relationship with God.

F = FORGIVENESS
The only solution to man's isolation and separation from a holy God is forgiveness. *"For Christ also suffered for sins once for all, the righteous for the unrighteous, that He might bring you to God, after being put to death in the fleshly realm but made alive in the spiritual realm"* (1 Pet. 3:18).

The only way our relationship can be restored with God is through the forgiveness of our sins. Jesus Christ died on the cross for this very purpose.

E = ETERNAL LIFE
You can have full and abundant life in this present life . . . and eternal life when you die. *"But to all who did receive Him, He gave them the right to be children of God, to those who believe in His name"* (John 1:12). *"A thief comes only to steal and to kill and to destroy. I have come that they may have life and have it in abundance"* (John 10:10).

Is there any reason you wouldn't like to have a personal relationship with God?

THE PLAN OF SALVATION

It's as simple as ABC. All you have to do is:

A = Admit you are a sinner. Turn from your sin and turn to God. *"Repent and turn back, that your sins may be wiped out so that seasons of refreshing may come from the presence of the Lord"* (Acts 3:19).

B = Believe that Jesus died for your sins and rose from the dead enabling you to have life. *"I have written these things to you who believe in the name of the Son of God, so that you may know that you have eternal life"* (1 John 5:13).

C = Confess verbally and publicly your belief in Jesus Christ. *"If you confess with your mouth, 'Jesus is Lord,' and believe in your heart that God raised Him from the dead, you will be saved. With the heart one believes, resulting in righteousness, and with the mouth one confesses, resulting in salvation"* (Rom. 10:9–10).

You can invite Jesus Christ to come into your life right now. Pray something like this:

"God, I admit that I am a sinner. I believe that you sent Jesus, who died on the cross and rose from the dead, paying the penalty for my sins. I am asking that you forgive me of my sin, and I receive your gift of eternal life. It is in Jesus' name that I ask for this gift. Amen."

Signed _____

Date _____

If you have a friend or family member who is a Christian, tell them about your decision. Then find a church that teaches the Bible, and let them help you go deeper with Christ.

KINGDOM PROMISES

If you've enjoyed this book of Kingdom Promises, you may want to consider reading one of the others in the series:

God Is
978-0-8054-4766-8

God Will
978-0-8054-4768-2

We Are
978-0-8054-2783-7

We Can
978-0-8054-2780-6

But God
978-0-8054-2782-0

Available in stores nationwide and through major online retailers. For a complete look at Ken Hemphill titles, make sure to visit www.bhpublishinggroup.com/hemphill or auxanopress.com/catalog.

SPLASH

SHOW PEOPLE LOVE AND SHARE HIM

BY KEN & PAULA HEMPHILL

Would you like to reach your
community the way Jesus reached his?

The most *economical* and *effective*
evangelism program available.

splashinfo.com
Follow on Twitter: SplashZone

Now available…

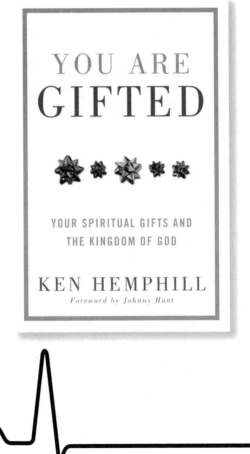

YOU ARE
GIFTED

YOUR SPIRITUAL GIFTS AND
THE KINGDOM OF GOD

KEN HEMPHILL
Foreword by Johnny Hunt

An EKG Resource